A Question of Science

Can You Hear Sounds in Space?

HELLO?

And other questions about **SOUND**

Anna Claybourne

CRABTREE
PUBLISHING COMPANY
WWW.CRABTREEBOOKS.COM

CRABTREE
PUBLISHING COMPANY
WWW.CRABTREEBOOKS.COM

Published in Canada
Crabtree Publishing
616 Welland Ave.
St. Catharines, Ontario
L2M 5V6

Published in the United States
Crabtree Publishing
347 Fifth Avenue
Suite 1402–145
New York, NY 10016

Published in 2021 by Crabtree Publishing Company

First published in 2020 by Wayland
© Hodder and Stoughton 2020

Author: Anna Claybourne

Editorial Director: Kathy Middleton

Editor: Julia Bird

Proofreader: Petrice Custance

Design and illustration: Matt Lilly

Cover design: Matt Lilly

Production coordinator and
  Prepress technician: Tammy McGarr

Print coordinator: Katherine Berti

Printed in the U.S.A./082020/CG20200601

Picture credits
Alamy: Dorling Kindersley Ltd 11cr; Science History Images 14t.
Getty Images: Kevork Djansezian 22br.
iStock: Aleksandar Georgiev 4b.
NASA: cover, 1, 8t, 8b.
Nature PL: Valeriy Maleev 26t.
Shutterstock: Annet999 4tc; Natalia Bachkova 6c; Bergamont 11b; Thorsten Bock 17cr; Champion studio 5tr; Donna Ellen Coleman 4c; Dwi putra stock 16br, 17br; eNjoy iStyle 5tc; 5 second studio 17bc; Eric Isselee 17tl, 17bcl; Kamnuan 5tl; Luka Kikina 25t; Leungchopan 28t; Yan Lev 20t; Boris Medvedev 16bl; Megaflopp 4tl; Mega Pixel 16tr; Nomad Photo Reference 9t; Ozanuysal 19c; Tatiana Popova 19t; Andrey_Popov 22bl; Janos Rautonen 29b; Rumo 29c; Sarah2 18b; Sashkin 23t; SeaTops/Imagebroker 20b;Skycolors 12c;Yuliia Sonsedska 4tr; Preju Suresh 27t; 3DMI 24b; Denis Trofimov 11cl; Joost van Uffelen 11t;VanderWolf Images 17bl; Peter Verreussel 26c; Milan Zygmunt 27c.
US Navy Photo: Mass Communications Specialist 3rd Class, Travis K Mendoza 12t.

Library and Achives Canada Cataloguing in Publication

Title: Can you hear sounds in space? : and other questions about sound / Anna Claybourne.
Names: Claybourne, Anna, author.
Description: Series statement: A question of science | Includes index.
Identifiers: Canadiana (print) 20200255762 | Canadiana (ebook) 20200255800 | ISBN 9780778777496 (softcover) | ISBN 9780778777052 (hardcover) | ISBN 9781427125378 (PDF)
Subjects: LCSH: Sound—Juvenile literature. | LCSH: Sound—Miscellanea—Juvenile literature. | LCGFT: Trivia and miscellanea.
Classification: LCC QC225.5 .C53 2020 | DDC j534—dc23

Library of Congress Cataloging-in-Publication Data

Names: Claybourne, Anna, author.

Title: Can you hear sounds in space? : and other questions about sound / Anna Claybourne.
Description: New York, NY : Crabtree Publishing Company, 2021. | Series: A question of science | First published in 2020 by Wayland.
Identifiers: LCCN 2020023617 (print) | LCCN 2020023618 (ebook) | ISBN 9780778777052 (hardcover) | ISBN 9780778777496 (paperback) | ISBN 9781427125378 (ebook)
Subjects: LCSH: Sound--Juvenile literature.
Classification: LCC QC225.5 .C558 2021 (print) | LCC QC225.5 (ebook) | DDC 534--dc23
LC record available at https://lccn.loc.gov/2020023617
LC ebook record available at https://lccn.loc.gov/2020023618

Contents

What is sound?

Wherever we are, sound is all around us.

DING DING DING DING!

TOOT! TOOT!

MEOW!

VROOOOOM!

There's always something making a noise, whether it's traffic, music, people chatting, a clock ticking, or just your own breathing. But where does sound come from? What's actually happening when something like a drum or an ambulance makes a noise?

Sound is movement

Sound is a kind of **energy**, like light, heat, and movement. In fact, sound IS a type of movement energy. Here's what happens.

BANG! BANG! TAP TAP! BANG!

The player hits the drum.

The drum skin vibrates, or moves quickly back and forth.

The vibrating drum pushes the air around it.

The air starts to vibrate in the same pattern.

The vibrations spread out through the air in waves, called **sound waves.**

4

Sensing sounds

Most animals, including humans, have **evolved** the ability to sense sounds by detecting the vibrations in the air.

Snakes don't have ears like ours, but they can sense sound vibrations with their bodies.

We use the sound-collecting **organs** on our heads—our ears!.

PARDON?

Crickets hear using organs called tympani on their front legs.

Handy hearing

Hearing is incredibly useful. It can warn us of danger or help us find things.

CRACK!

UH OH!

We use it to communicate by talking. We also use it for fun, in the form of music and dancing.

The sound of silence

Even when you think it's "quiet," there's still sound. For example, in a "quiet" library you can still hear whispering, book pages turning, distant traffic, wind, or your own breathing.

Scientists have been able to build a soundproof room that is almost totally silent and has no **echoes**. Called an **anechoic** room, no one really finds it peaceful and relaxing! Instead, being in an anechoic room can make you feel scared, confused, or even sick. Most people's brains aren't used to silence and can't cope with it!

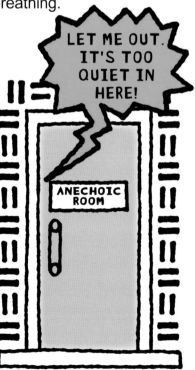

LET ME OUT. IT'S TOO QUIET IN HERE!

ANECHOIC ROOM

How do sounds get inside your ears?

The air is full of sound waves coming at us from many different directions. Somehow, we can hear them all at the same time and make sense of them.

So what really happens when sound waves reach your ears?

How can pieces of air wobbling back and forth tell you that there's a bird singing, a car coming, or that your friend is calling your name?

① Sound waves

③ Sound waves travel along the ear canal.

② The outer ear, or pinna, collects sound waves and directs them into the ear opening.

Inside your ears

You might think your ears are just those flappy things on the sides of your head, but there's a lot more to them than that! They actually reach deep inside your skull, where they connect to your brain.

Making sense of sounds

Inside the brain, the sound signals are sent to the auditory cortex. This is the area of the brain that deals with sound.

Auditory cortex

WATCH OUT, A CAR'S COMING!

IS THAT JOSH OVER THERE?

It figures out what the patterns of vibrations mean by comparing them to its memories of sounds.

④ The moving air hits the **eardrum**, a tightly stretched **membrane** or skin, making it vibrate.

⑤ The vibrations pass through three tiny bones called the anvil, hammer, and stirrup...

⑥ ... and into the **cochlea**, a snail-shaped space in the skull. The vibrations spread through a liquid inside the cochlea. This makes tiny hairs vibrate.

⑦ The hairs turn the vibrations into electrical signals. The signals travel along **nerves** into the brain.

It's all vibrations!

Amazingly, everything you can hear is just different patterns of vibrations. You can show sound wave patterns as graphs, like this:

Someone talking

Dog barking

Music

Even if you hear all these patterns together, your brain can sort the sounds out and tell which is which.

Can you hear sounds in space?

Well, yes and no. It depends where you are! For example, astronauts on the International Space Station (ISS) can hear each other talking, and even enjoy playing music to relax.

But if you were floating in outer space, you wouldn't be able to hear any sounds at all.

Astronaut Edward T. Lu plays the keyboard—upside down! —on board the ISS.

HELLO?

Where's the air?

On Earth, you hear sounds because sound waves travel through the air. The air is made up of tiny gas **molecules**. Sound waves spread out through the air when the molecules move around and hit against each other. There's air inside the ISS, so sound works just like on Earth.

But in outer space, when you're not in a spacecraft, there isn't any air.

Most of space is empty, with very few molecules in it. So sound waves can't spread out from objects to your ears, and you can't hear anything.

Quiet Moon

It's the same on the Moon, since it doesn't have air or any other gases around it. It's silent there, too.

SILENCE IS GOLDEN!

MEOW!

Speeding through a medium

Sound waves need something known as a **medium** to travel through. The medium is often air or gas, but sounds can travel through liquids and solids, too.

That's why you can hear a cat meowing outside, for example. The sound waves travel through the air, but also through the window or door.

Without a medium, sound can't go anywhere.

HMMMM HMMMM HMMMMM!

Sounds of the Sun

Though we can't hear the Sun through space, it does vibrate.

Scientists have measured the vibrations using telescopes, and turned them into a sound that we can hear! It's a kind of rustling, humming noise.

Why can't you see sound waves?

When someone makes a sound and you hear it, that's because the sound waves have carried the sound energy toward you through the air.

GO REDSHIRTS!!

Invisible sound waves

But you don't see anything happening in the air in between.

There are two main reasons for this:

① You can't see air

Sound waves happen when tiny air molecules move back and forth and push against each other. If you could see them, they would look a bit like this:

On a sound wave diagram like this, the pressed-together areas are shown as peaks.

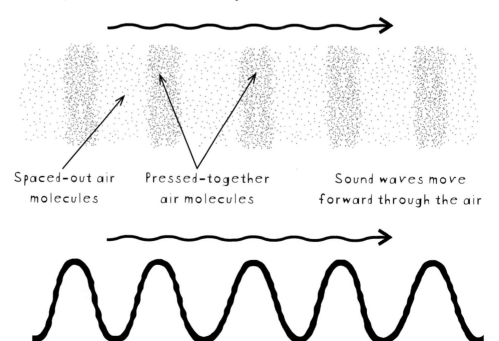

Spaced-out air molecules

Pressed-together air molecules

Sound waves move forward through the air

② It's too fast

Even in a liquid or a solid, it's hard to see sound waves because the movements of the molecules are too fast for our eyes to keep up.

Dolphins make a lot of sounds underwater to "talk" to each other. We can't see the sound waves vibrating in the water.

Good vibes...

However, we can see objects vibrating as they make sound. This is a good way to get an idea of what sound waves are like.

When you pluck a guitar string, you can see it vibrate very fast, making it look blurry. The string's vibration makes the air move, which creates the sound waves. You just can't see the sound waves.

A bell or cymbal that's just been bonged vibrates with sound, too.

Sound in action

See the action of sound waves with this experiment.

Stretch a piece of plastic wrap tightly over a bowl.

Sprinkle a few grains of sugar or salt onto the middle.

Carefully put the bowl next to a stereo or radio speaker...

BOOM!

BOOM!

... and put on some loud music. What happens?

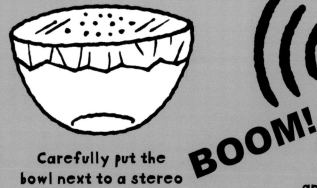

How fast is a supersonic plane?

An F/A-18C Hornet supersonic jet breaking the **sound barrier**

BOOM!

Supersonic means fast!

A supersonic plane can fly faster than the speed of sound itself. And when that happens, there's a VERY loud noise.

The speed of sound in air, depending on the temperature, is around 767 mph (1,234 kph).

Passenger aircraft usually fly at less than 621 mph (1,000 kph).

WAIT FOR ME!

A Boeing 747 isn't a supersonic plane. It's too slow!

Sonic BOOM!

Supersonic (faster than sound) planes are usually fighter jets or scientific aircraft, not passenger planes. A loud **sonic boom** happens when the plane catches up with the speed of sound.

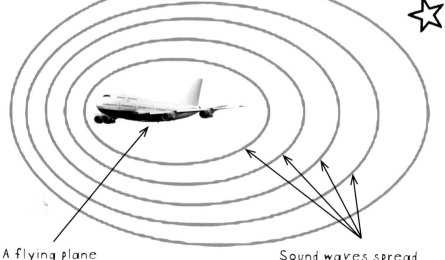

A flying plane makes sound.

Sound waves spread outward from the plane.

When a plane flies faster than sound, its own sound waves can't keep up with it.

The sound waves "pile up" and join together behind the plane, making an extra big, loud sound wave.

BOOM!

What's that cone-shaped cloud?

The huge sound wave creates an area of low **air pressure**. This makes water in the air **condense** into droplets in a cone-shaped mini-cloud, called a vapor cone.

On the ground, you hear a noise like thunder, called a sonic boom.

How many Mach?

Supersonic pilots talk about speed in **Mach** numbers.

Mach 1 means your speed is the same as the speed of sound in the air you're flying through.

NEEEEEOOWWW!

MACH 1! WE HAVE MACH 1!

CRUISING AT MACH 1.5...

Mach 1.5 is 1.5 times the speed of sound.

NASA's X-15 rocket plane reached Mach 6.7—that's 6.7 times the speed of sound, or 4,520 mph (7,274kph)!

THWACK!

That's not fast!

Sound seems fast, but compared to light, it's a snail's pace!

Speed of light 670,616,629 mph (1,079,252,848 kph) If someone hits a ball 985 feet (300 m) away from you, the light reaches your eyes almost immediately. But the sound arrives almost a second later.

13

What was the loudest sound ever?

BANG!

On August 27, 1883, the volcanic island of Krakatoa in Indonesia exploded in an enormous eruption, making one of the loudest sounds in history.

WHAT WAS THAT?

OWWW, MY EARS!

The noise was so loud, it burst the eardrums of sailors on a ship called the *Norham Castle*—40 miles (65 km) away!

As far as 100 miles (160 km) away, the sound of the eruption was measured at 172 **decibels** (db). That's louder than a rocket taking off right next to you! And people as far as 3,107 miles (5,000 km) away heard it, too.

Up close, the eruption may have measured up to 310 decibels.

What makes sounds loud?

As you know, sounds can be quiet or loud. You can shout or whisper. You can turn the **volume** on a radio or TV up and down. The loudness of a sound is decided by its intensity. That means how much energy it carries.

The louder a sound is, the more the molecules move and the harder they hit your eardrums. That's why a really loud sound hurts your ears because it's hitting your eardrums really hard!

In a quieter sound, the molecules in the air move back and forth a little way as the sound waves pass by.

A quieter sound is shown as a smaller wave.

In a louder sound, they move farther and faster.

A louder sound contains more energy and is shown as a bigger wave.

Deafening decibels

We measure sound intensity on the decibel scale. On the decibel scale, a measurment of 20 is 10 times louder than 10, 30 is 10 times louder than 20, and so on.

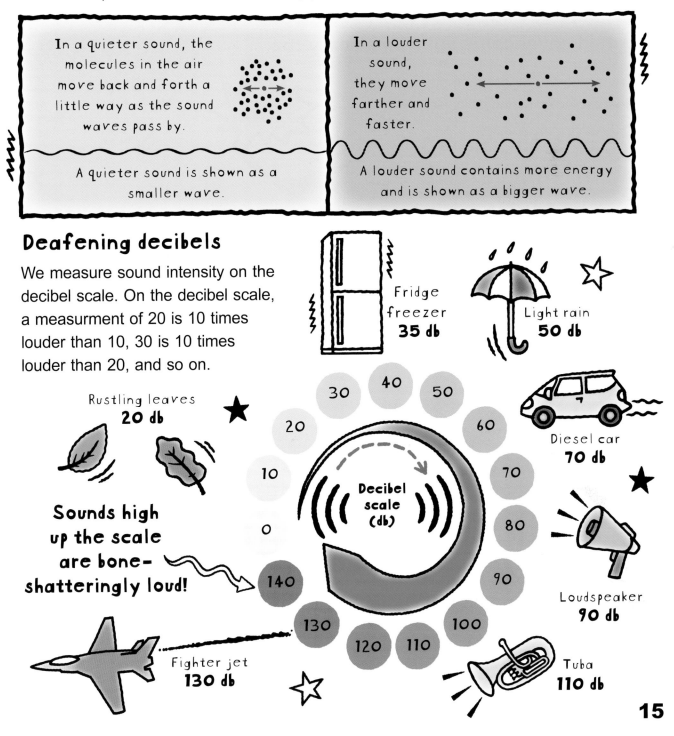

Fridge freezer
35 db

Light rain
50 db

Rustling leaves
20 db

Sounds high up the scale are bone-shatteringly loud!

Decibel scale (db)

Diesel car
70 db

Loudspeaker
90 db

Tuba
110 db

Fighter jet
130 db

15

Why do lions roar but mice squeak? ☆

SQUEAK!

When a lion is annoyed, you don't expect it to squeak at you! And a mouse would never come out with a scary roar.

We're used to bigger animals making deeper, lower-sounding noises.

ROAR!

It's the same with musical instruments.

PARP!

PARP!

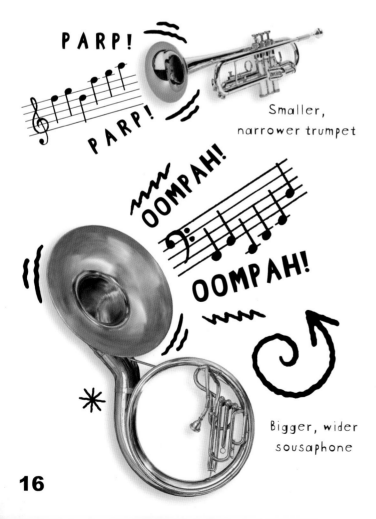

Smaller, narrower trumpet

OOMPAH!

OOMPAH!

Bigger, wider sousaphone

High and low

The "highness" or "lowness" of a sound is called its pitch.

Pitch is decided by the **frequency** of sound waves, or how close together (or frequent) they are. The higher the frequency, the higher the sound.

Frequency is usually measured in **hertz** (sound waves per second).

Music has notes of different pitches. Like music, we vary our pitch when speaking.

High-pitched sound Low-pitched sound ★ ☆

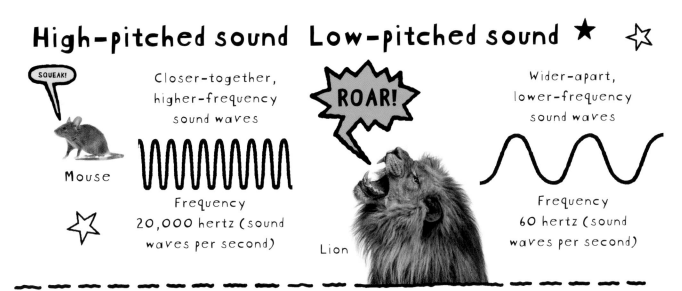

SQUEAK!

Mouse

Closer-together, higher-frequency sound waves

Frequency 20,000 hertz (sound waves per second)

ROAR!

Lion

Wider-apart, lower-frequency sound waves

Frequency 60 hertz (sound waves per second)

Vibration speed

If an object vibrates quickly, it creates more frequent sound waves, resulting in a higher-pitched sound. Smaller, shorter objects tend to vibrate faster and make higher-pitched sounds, while bigger, longer ones vibrate more slowly, and make lower-pitched sounds.

For example, when you play a guitar, you shorten the string to make a higher note.

MOOOO!

ROAR!

MEOW!

SQUEAK!

Cow   Lion   Cat Mouse

Animals make sounds using their vocal cords or other parts in their throats. The smaller the animal, the smaller its body parts and the more likely it is to make a high, squeaky sound.

Changing your voice

Pitch is incredibly important in how we speak and communicate. See for yourself!

Use pitch to give the word "no" different meanings, such as:

An amazed "No!"
An angry "No."
A questioning "No?"

Where do sound waves go?

When you make a sound, by clapping your hands, for example, the sound is gone soon afterward. It doesn't keep traveling around the world forever.

(In fact, if sound did just hang around like that, the world would be impossibly noisy. We'd still be hearing all the sounds ever made!)

So what happens to it?

Spreading out

When something makes a sound, sound waves start spreading out from it in all directions. As they spread out, they get fainter.

② As the waves get farther away, they must cover a bigger area.

③ But there's still only the same amount of sound energy, so it gets spread out.

① Near to the sound source, it's easier to hear.

④ Someone standing farther away hears a fainter sound.

The sound is gone!

Although sounds go away, they cannot just vanish. Sound is a kind of energy, and energy can only be changed into other types of energy. As sound makes molecules in the air move, it actually heats up the air slightly. Eventually, as the sound waves spread out, all the sound energy gets turned into heat.

It's only a tiny amount of heat, though—not enough to feel!

Soaking up sound

Sounds can also disappear when they hit something, especially a soft surface like a cushion.

The sound waves hit the molecules in the cushion and make them move. This turns the sound energy into heat energy, and the cushion heats up slightly.

Soundproofed rooms are lined with materials that are good at soaking up sounds, such as squishy foam.

Foam on headphones soaks up sounds from outside, helping you to hear what you are listening to more clearly.

ECHO-CHO-CHO...

When sound waves hit a hard, smooth surface though, they can bounce off, making an echo. Stone, brick, and concrete reflect sound well.

You shout...

HELLOOOO!

HELLOOOO!

The wall echoes the sound back to you.

Why is it hard to hear underwater?

If you and a friend jump into a swimming pool, then put your heads under the water and try to have a chat, it's not going to work very well.

But whales and dolphins can hear each other underwater without a problem.

What's going on?

Sound in water

Sound does actually travel well underwater. It travels more than four times faster in water than in air.

MRRRR! MMMMMMMMRRR!*

*Translation: I'm over here!

A lot of sea creatures use sound and hearing to hunt, communicate, and find a mate—just like this leopard seal.